2025–2026 Prayer Journal

THIS JOURNAL BELONGS TO

Living with Christ

Publisher: David Dziena
Associate Publisher: Father John Franck, A.A.
Editor: Terence Hegarty
Project Editor: Michelle Gerstel
Design: Jeff McCall

Sponsored by the Augustinians of the Assumption
Provincial: Father Chi Ai Nguyen, A.A.

Bayard, Inc.
500 Salisbury St. ■ Worcester, MA 01609
PHONE: (800) 214-3386
WEBSITE: www.livingwithchrist.us
EMAIL: LWC@bayardfaithresources.com

ISBN: 978-1-62785-842-7
Printed in the U.S.A.

The best guide you can find
to the correct spiritual path
is the serious study of the

BIBLE.

There we can find rules
for the conduct of our life
and, in the lives of the great figures,
living images of a life with God
whose actions we are
encouraged to copy.

ST. BASIL THE GREAT

WHY JOURNAL?

Spiritual journaling is a form of prayer. Far beyond recapping our life's events, the exercise of journaling helps us to express our spiritual life. Our written words capture our spiritual experiences, thoughts, struggles, victories—and essentially form a prayer through which we communicate to God what lies in our innermost self.

The exercise of spiritual journaling does not require us to be experienced in such a practice, nor are there any specific guidelines. When we journal, we need not worry about style or formalities. Just as in our regular prayers, Jesus wishes us to speak freely, simply, and honestly what is in our heart.

This journal provides a guideline to your prayer exercise in the **Responding to the Word** section each day, where you will find a question that is directly connected to the readings of the day. If this question is helpful, feel free to use it, but do not feel constrained by it.

Spiritual journaling will essentially enlarge our vision and lead to a greater understanding of our spiritual journey.

PRAYER *for* *the* HELP *of the* HOLY SPIRIT

Come, Holy Spirit,
fill the hearts of your faithful
and kindle in them the fire
    of your love.
Send forth your Spirit
and they shall be created,
and you shall renew the face
    of the earth.
O God, who by the light
    of the Holy Spirit,
did instruct the hearts
    of the faithful,
grant that by the same Holy Spirit
we may be truly wise
and ever enjoy his consolations.
Through the same Christ Our Lord.

AMEN.

1ST SUNDAY *of* ADVENT

The first reading of this new liturgical year opens with "The word that Isaiah son of Amoz saw." This reminds me of a bumper sticker I've seen that reads "Visualize peace." Isaiah saw a message from God: a vision of peace, a time when people would turn swords into ploughshares, and no one would "learn war" any more. Of course, it takes more than visualizing. That's part of Paul's message in the second reading: to "wake from sleep"—not just to dream about doing good, but to put our dreams into practice. "The day is near," Paul says. There are things that should not be put off, opportunities for good that shouldn't be missed. In the gospel, too, is this sense of urgency: "Keep awake… for you do not know on what day your Lord is coming." As both Paul and Jesus insist, we don't know how much time we have, so we must be prepared to act. We can't just dream.

We must go beyond visualizing peace to actually working for peace. What are the steps we can take, the attitudes we can adopt, the organizations we can support, the lessons we can learn in the cause of peace?

For the Church, Advent is the beginning of a new year. This year, let us make a new year's resolution to become more fully people of peace. **DINAH SIMMONS**

Responding *to the* Word

Paul tells us to put aside godless ways and live in God's light. *What attitude or action should I reject this Advent?*

Final Thoughts...

FEASTS THIS WEEK

December 3: **St. Francis Xavier**

December 4: **St. John Damascene**

December 6: **St. Nicholas**

2ND SUNDAY *of* **ADVENT**

Today we meet John the Baptist in the wilderness. Matthew's gospel introduces him without any explanation because no introduction was needed. He was a great figure in the Jewish world of his day, not only in Judea but right across the Mediterranean. In the Acts of the Apostles (19.1-7), Paul comes across a group of John's disciples in Ephesus in what is today Turkey.

In one way, John was a deeply traditional figure in Judaism; in another way, he was a radical, new figure. He dressed like the prophet Elijah and went out, like Elijah, into the wilderness, calling people back to the word of God. In several places in the gospels, people in fact compare him with Elijah. In another way, he was very new because he called people to repent of their sins and be baptized as a sign of their repentance. The popularity of his challenging message, which drew great crowds out into the desert for baptism, shows that the time was ripe for the message of Jesus.

Jesus completed what John began: he offered a baptism in the Holy Spirit for the forgiveness of sins and the start of a new age of peace. In a sinful and dangerous world, we yearn for that gift of the Spirit promised by Isaiah in today's first reading, proclaimed by John in his ministry, and brought to fulfillment by Jesus.

JENNIFER COOPER

Responding *to the* Word

John encourages us to change our lives to prepare for Jesus' coming. ***What changes do I need to make this Advent?***

Final Thoughts...

FEASTS THIS WEEK

December 8: **The Immaculate Conception
of the Blessed Virgin Mary**

December 9: **St. Juan Diego Cuauhtlatoatzin**

December 10: **Our Lady of Loreto**

December 11: **St. Damasus I**

December 12: **Our Lady of Guadalupe**

December 13: **St. Lucy**

IMMACULATE CONCEPTION
of the BLESSED VIRGIN MARY

Mary, Mother of God, is often a larger-than-life figure for us, a woman set apart, honored for her "yes," her receptivity to divine mystery. But in today's gospel we meet a surprised and confused young woman who is initially overwhelmed and reluctant to accept her call. This very human response is one that we, as fellow disciples, can understand; we know it from our own relationship with God.

Mary's story is so familiar that perhaps we don't relate it to our experience. We see the Nativity as historically grounded, over and done with, and so we wonder what her "yes" might say to us. Unlike Mary, we are not usually visited by angels with requests from God. We are not called, we think, to give birth.

Yet according to some mystics and theologians in our tradition, Mary's story continues among us. Her pregnancy, they suggest, symbolizes the process of discipleship: it mirrors our own service. With her we are called to bring new life into our world. Our passion for justice, our desire to alleviate suffering, to support the poor, the homeless and the abused, to teach, to heal, to create, to nurture are calls from God inviting receptivity, reflection and response.

Imitating Mary's courage, may we continue to give birth to Christ, to Love, in our time and place. ❧ ELLA ALLEN

Responding *to the* Word

The angel tells Mary that nothing is impossible with God. ***When has God made the impossible possible in my life?***

Final Thoughts...

3RD SUNDAY *of* ADVENT

At the beginning of Sunday Mass, Father Jim calls the young children up to the altar. He gathers them around, then asks a question or two before sending them down to the church hall for their Sunday School.

One Advent Sunday he put a simple question to them: "Why does Jesus come at Christmas?" Without hesitation one four year old spoke up: "To make Jesus real."

A simple but powerful thought. Can we make Jesus real for our children, a true presence in the world around us and alive in our own hearts this Advent? Do we live in joyous expectation of his coming by seeking justice for the oppressed? Do we patiently anticipate his return by giving bread to the hungry and upholding the widow and orphan, as the psalmist says the Lord will do?

Or are we blinded to the needs around us by the self-absorbing consumerism of our society? Do we leave outstretched hands straining toward us untouched? If so, when will our eyes be opened? Does our deafness to the pleas of the persecuted across our planet mean that their cries go unanswered? When will our ears be unsealed?

The prophet Isaiah urges us to take heart, weary and feeble as we are when confronted by a world that denies the Lord. Whatever the obstacles, it is our duty to make Jesus real this Advent.

MICHAEL DOUGHERTY

Responding *to the* Word

John prepares a way for Jesus to draw near to us. ***What can I do today to smooth a way for God to come to others?***

Final Thoughts...

4TH SUNDAY *of* **ADVENT**

Even very young children know that being a king or queen is something remarkable. All that power! All those jewels and crowns and thrones and servants! Kings and queens are born of kings and queens, generation after generation. Except in today's gospel, that is.

Instead of being born of a human royal couple, Jesus, the Messiah, is to be born to a teenage girl and a laborer who isn't his father. This surprising story of Jesus' family tree turns our ideas about kingship upside down. The intriguing details about Jesus' conception and birth are the first of many signs of big changes in how we understand God. This long-awaited king is born in modest circumstances, with no earthly power, no jewels or crowns or thrones, no servants. In fact, as we know, this king becomes a servant to all.

Instead of being remote from the people, living in luxury, this king—Jesus, Emmanuel—lives as one of us. God is with us in the chaos and sadness and joy and messiness of our lives, not looking down from on high, but here on the ground, among us. As the story unfolds, we come to see Jesus as the model king: humble, compassionate, prayerful, loving, willing to sacrifice life itself for the good of the people. With the psalmist, we call for the Lord to enter, for truly he is king of glory. **ANNE LOUISE MAHONEY**

Responding *to the* Word

Joseph overcomes his fear to accept Jesus' growth in Mary's womb. ***What fears make it hard for me to accept Jesus' growing presence in me?***

Final Thoughts...

NATIVITY *of the* LORD (CHRISTMAS)

Take a moment to remember a Christmas celebration that was deeply meaningful…

The Christmases of deepest meaning for me took place where there was no snow, Christmas tree decorations, family, fruit cake, or eggnog. When I lived in Latin America, I spent three Christmases picking coffee in the mountains, sleeping on the schoolhouse floor, and eating only rice, tortillas, and beans. We worked to assist peasant cooperatives bring in their harvest, the best of which was exported to North America.

One year, as we celebrated Christmas by preparing a piñata game for the kids of the community, we received word that a baby had died. Visiting the simple hut of the grieving family, we discovered that due to unsanitary living conditions—no running water, no electricity, no medical care—worms had infected and eventually killed the infant.

Thousands of years before, a young virgin mother gave birth in similar conditions, wrapped her firstborn son in swaddling rags and laid him in a manger because there was no place for them in the inn. Mary's heart must have been breaking to have had to receive the Son of God in this manner, and yet the new mother was no doubt also bursting with joy. Christmas is a time to open our hearts to God. This Christmas let us also resolve to make room in our hearts for all the children of the world.

JOSEPH GUNN

____

____

____

____

READINGS
OF THE DAY

Mass during the Night

Isaiah 9.2-4, 6-7

Psalm 96

Titus 2.11-14

Luke 2.1-16

Mass at Dawn

Isaiah 62.11-12

Psalm 97

Titus 3.4-7

Luke 2.15-20

Mass during the Day

Isaiah 52.7-10

Psalm 98

Hebrews 1.1-6

John 1.1-18

Responding *to the* Word

Isaiah foresees the beginning of freedom from our burdens. *What burdens do I want Jesus to lift from me today?*

Final Thoughts...

HOLY FAMILY *of* JESUS, MARY *and* JOSEPH

We all have our roots in a family. When we become adults we often spend our lives trying to establish another family like our own, or one that is radically different. Either way, the family in which we are raised shapes our vision of what a family should be.

Today's readings invite us to reflect on families other than our own. Above all, we celebrate the Holy Family as a model, both for biological families and for the spiritual family that is the community of faith. The gospel focuses on Joseph's willingness to sacrifice his own desires and comfort for the sake of his newborn son. Mary is mentioned almost in passing here, but she too willingly accepted God's will for her in bearing the Son within her.

The other two readings also describe the ideal family. Sirach provides guidelines for how children should interact with their parents, especially as their parents age. This expands upon the fourth commandment ("Honor your father and mother"), which was addressed to adults, not children. In Colossians Paul starts by telling us how to relate to one another as members of the Christian community, then makes these principles concrete by applying them to the family itself.

The message running through these readings is the call to give greater attention to the needs of others. If we give our lives in service of others then we will be creating the family that God desires—in our families, our parish, our church, our community, and, through them, in the entire world. An idealistic plan, yes, but the readings and the Lord who inspired them call us to nothing less. **JOHN L. MCLAUGHLIN**

Responding *to the* Word

Joseph must protect his vulnerable wife and child. ***What can I do today to help mothers and children who need help and protection?***

Final Thoughts...

FEASTS THIS WEEK

December 29: **St. Thomas Becket**

December 31: **St. Sylvester I**

January 1: **Mary, the Holy Mother of God**

January 2: **St. Basil the Great
& St. Gregory Nazianzen**

January 3: **The Most Holy Name of Jesus**

MARY, *the* HOLY MOTHER *of* GOD
World Day of Peace

One woman changed the world. Today we celebrate Mary, woman of faith, woman of peace, whose radical "yes" transformed the world. Who is this woman we call "Mary, Mother of God"?

Mary held an open stance toward God, toward life, enabling her to face the challenges of her courageous "yes" to God. She was able to live with mystery. As a devout Jew, Mary listened to God's voice, discerning God's will for her. Her openness, love for God, and courage to endure misunderstanding led this young woman to take a great risk and change the course of human history. Her strength came from the depth of her being. In today's gospel, Luke says Mary "treasured all these words" and "pondered them in her heart." She lived the freedom of the spirit we all desire. This freedom came from the realization that God was with her through the pain and joy of her decision.

On this World Day of Peace, we have much to learn about peace from Mary. To bring peace to our world we must listen to God speaking to us in the events of the day, to voices from different cultures and religions, and to those with whom we disagree.

By reflecting on the word of God and the words of those around us we can deepen the peace within and, like Mary, help to fashion a more peaceful world.   SR. JUDY MORRIS, OP

Responding *to the* Word

Mary reflected on all the ways God worked in her life. *How will I thank God for being present in my life this past year?*

Final Thoughts...

EPIPHANY *of the* LORD

The Wise Men are a standard feature of our Christmas traditions. They appear in seasonal pageants and Nativity scenes, greeting cards and decorations, stories old and new, even jokes. Surprisingly perhaps, their only appearance in Scripture is this account in the Gospel of Matthew. Even here the details are sparse: no royal robes, no camels, indeed no mention of a threesome of travelers.

Based on this single scriptural reference, then, what do we actually know about these visitors? They are apparently learned and intelligent men, and—judging from the gifts they bring—also wealthy. What is clear is that their journey has been challenging, with its exact length and ultimate destination unknown to them at the outset. They set forth with no map and no clear directions, only their faith in the beckoning light of an unusual star.

At journey's end, they find a scene of poverty and simplicity. Far from being disappointed or discouraged, however, they are overjoyed. The uncertainties and problems of the journey are forgotten as they gaze in awe at the child before them.

Deep within ourselves, we too feel the pull of that star, the call to journey God-ward in faith. More often than not, the road ahead is unclear; we may be distracted by detours and difficulties or the deceitful voices of the Herods in our midst. Matthew's faithful seekers, traveling together in search of truth, are models for our own journey of faith. **KRYSTYNA HIGGINS**

Responding *to the* Word

The magi left their familiar environment to seek and honor a Jewish king. *How am I being drawn to discover God in new places and situations?*

Final Thoughts...

FEASTS THIS WEEK

January 5: **St. John Neumann**
January 6: **St. André Bessette**
January 7: **St. Raymond of Penyafort**

BAPTISM *of the* LORD

Have you ever attended a blessing of the Easter fire outdoors? How carefully we cradle and protect from the wind the dimly burning flame as we pass it through the congregation! How conscious of and attentive we are to those around us trying to do the same thing. What joy we experience! All because we are caught up in something much bigger than ourselves—God's will from all time for the achievement of our salvation.

Israel, as God's chosen servant, was commissioned to care for all people in just this same gentle, attentive, and joyous way. Despite its terrible experience of exile in Babylon, Israel must now be a light to the nations in steadfast obedience to the righteous will of God until the justice, enlightenment, and freedom intended by that divine will for all humanity are fully accomplished.

Matthew knew Isaiah's first Servant Song well and thought it applied perfectly to Jesus. Here was a devout Jew, a representative of Israel, whose messiahship was as gentle as it was powerful and whose obedience to the Father's will was without flaw. Having no need of John's baptism, Jesus joins us in our need of repentance, and invites John to cooperate with him to fulfill God's will.

At his baptism, Jesus is revealed as Beloved Son, Chosen Servant, Messiah, and King. At the same time, he stands in solidarity with each of us without partiality. Can gratitude for such a saving gift, promised from of old, also spur us on to be a faithful and willing covenant people? **CHRISTINE MADER**

Responding *to the* Word

At his baptism, Jesus is identified as God's beloved child. ***How did my baptism identify me as God's beloved child?***

Final Thoughts...

FEASTS THIS WEEK

January 13: **St. Hilary**
January 17: **St. Anthony**

2ND SUNDAY *in* ORDINARY TIME
Week of Prayer for Christian Unity

Who exactly is this Jesus whose birth, epiphany, and baptism we have so recently celebrated? And what enduring relevance has God's entry into time for us?

The voices of Isaiah, John the Baptist, and Paul witness to the identity and mission of the Word become flesh. Isaiah sets the context for the incarnation as he anticipates a servant who will bring light and salvation to all. John affirms Jesus as "Lamb of God," as Son whose intimacy with God enables him to baptize with the Holy Spirit. Grace and peace are God's gifts to us through Jesus, Paul teaches. Anticipation, promise, prophecy are realized in and through the person of Jesus.

Isaiah, John, and Paul speak out of their experience, out of their lived relationship with God. We too are called to relationship with God. It is rather startling to hear that our call is to be saints—not saints as perfect, idealized larger-than-life figures who are impossibly pious—but ordinary everyday people who live as Christ-bearers, who recognize the dignity of all people, and who continue God's mission of love and compassion to the poor, the marginalized, to those most in need of light and healing.

With Isaiah, John, and Paul we are called to witness, to testify to the light through our words, our actions, our lives. **ELLA ALLEN**

Responding *to the* Word

We are called to share in the task of bringing everyone to God. ***What can I do today to draw someone closer to God?***

Final Thoughts...

FEASTS THIS WEEK

January 20: **St. Fabian**
St. Sebastian

January 21: **St. Agnes**

January 22: **Day of Prayer for the Legal**
Protection of Unborn Children

January 23: **St. Vincent**
St. Marianne Cope

January 24: **St. Francis de Sales**

3RD SUNDAY *in* ORDINARY TIME
Sunday of the Word of God

Does it not strike you as amazing that Jesus calls on ordinary people to become his first disciples? Jesus wants them to join him in a new kind of community and to experience intimately a loving and faithful relationship with him and with each other. It is a call to proclaim "the good news of the kingdom" to all people they will encounter and minister to.

What would so profoundly influence their decision to become Jesus' first disciples? I believe it was their faith in and desire for the love of God that inspired them to bring love and hope to a dark world. They were being given the opportunity through God's gift of grace to change their ways and participate as a community in God's plan of love and salvation.

As we close the Week of Prayer for Christian Unity, let this gospel serve as a reminder that Jesus summons all of us to be in real relationship with him and with those around us. As Christians in community, let us listen to Paul who reminds us we are "united in the same mind and for the same purpose," to serve and care for those around us, especially for the poor. It is in communion with Jesus that our hope and promise of God's abundant grace are to be found—a pure gift for all of us. **JULIE CACHIA**

Responding *to the* Word

Isaiah reminds us that God's presence is often recognized in what has been overlooked or neglected. ***Who or what might I have not noticed that is a source of God's presence?***

Final Thoughts...

FEASTS THIS WEEK

January 26: **St. Timothy & St. Titus**
January 27 : **St. Angela Merici**
January 28: **St. Thomas Aquinas**
January 31: **St. John Bosco**

4TH SUNDAY *in* **ORDINARY TIME**

We seek glory because it is our human nature to do so. Self-seeking glory is all around us. God challenges us to recognize that God-in-us will lead to great things. God in our small, weak selves leads to holiness, a different glory. And though our culture shapes us, we shape our culture; the culture changes only when God shapes us. When Jesus taught the Beatitudes, he was challenging the culture, too.

Each one of Jesus' exhortations—*Blessed are…*—is a profound witness of faith and trust in someone greater than ourselves. Suffering the cost of living the Beatitudes shows the world a new way to live, one rooted in Christ. Can we be surprised that it will be exceedingly difficult to live this way? How shall we?

Here is how. God's love for us compels God to share God's divine nature with us through Christ. Does God need us to accomplish this plan? Not really. Does God invite us? Every day. Let us say "yes."

Rejoice, then, that Jesus can use us to teach the strong and, at times, humble them. Even in this, no one can boast, because we all share the same self-glorifying human nature. We are only our best selves when God's divine nature is at work in us. There is no glory for us when living the Beatitudes. All glory belongs to God.

JOHANNE BROWNRIGG

Responding *to the* Word

Zephaniah describes the behavior of those faithful to God's covenant demands. *Which of these behaviors might I need to adopt?*

Final Thoughts...

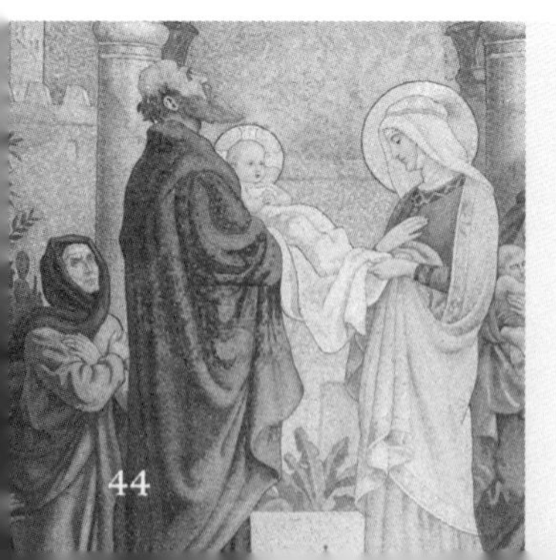

FEASTS THIS WEEK

February 2: **The Presentation of the Lord**

February 3: **St. Blaise**
St. Ansgar

February 5: **St. Agatha**

February 6: **St. Paul Miki & Companions**

5TH SUNDAY *in* **ORDINARY TIME**

Imagine a world without salt, without light—dull, dark, insipid, and lifeless. How often we take for granted these simple gifts of salt and light, symbols we ponder today as we reflect on the meaning of Christian discipleship.

For the people of Jesus' time, salt was essential in a world without refrigeration. Its most delightful quality, though, is its ability to enhance the flavor of foods—not to give them a different taste, but to bring out the taste that is already there. A light is first and foremost something to be seen or it is of not use, just as salt without flavor is useless.

These images of salt and light are part of Jesus' Sermon on the Mount, spoken to those who lack material goods and wait for the spiritual blessings promised by God. It is a happiness that reaches its fulfillment through Christ. This is not law. It is gospel, good news. The law challenges us to rely on our best efforts. The gospel confronts us with God's gifts and invites us to claim them as the basis for our life.

By our baptism, we are the light that shines in the darkness. We are the salt that gives new life to the world. This is what we celebrate in Eucharist today.

SR. MARY ELLEN GREEN, OP

Responding *to the* Word

God commands us to feed the hungry and satisfy the afflicted. ***In what ways am I meeting the needs of my community?***

READINGS OF THE DAY

Isaiah 58.6-10

Psalm 112

1 Corinthians 2.1-5

Matthew 5.13-16

Final Thoughts...

6TH SUNDAY *in* ORDINARY TIME

Today's Scripture passages echo and re-echo the same essential concept. The verses of Psalm 119 will guide our response. "Give me understanding, that I may keep your law and observe it with my whole heart."

The reading from Matthew's gospel is packed with potential actions, optional responses, and possible consequences. "But I say to you" signals that the stakes are being raised to a whole new level. We find the same approach in the reading from Sirach: fire and water, life and death, good and evil. The Lord is not interested in half measures or lukewarm responses. Pick one or the other; there is no room here to sit on the fence. The message is unchanging: come to the Lord completely.

This should not surprise us, for it is from the One who chose to empty himself completely and become one of us to show us the way to God. It comes from the One who lived among us and then gave himself up to pain and death for us. It comes from the One who fully and absolutely understands what it is to be human.

And it comes with the promise that we can spend our whole life in a constant and profound relationship with divine grace and love, immersed in God forever.

MARILYN J. SWEET

Responding *to the* Word

Keeping God's commandments is a choice that we must make. ***What helps me to keep the commandments of God?***

Final Thoughts...

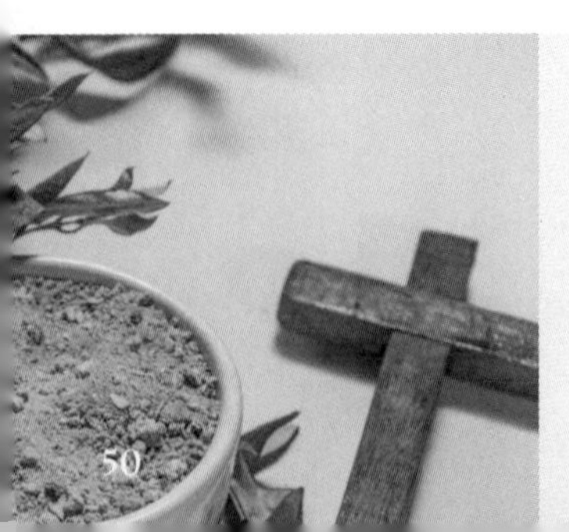

FEASTS THIS WEEK

February 17: **The Seven Holy Founders
of the Servite Order**

February 18: **Ash Wednesday**

February 21: **St. Peter Damian**

ASH WEDNESDAY

As we begin Lent we hear Jesus speaking of what we know to be three Lenten practices: almsgiving, prayer, and fasting. His words—which seem, at first hearing, to be a negative command: "Do not do these things in public"—are really an invitation to live in a way that expresses who we are as Christians.

Both the gospel and the first reading make it clear that our almsgiving, prayer, and fasting are not to be done to impress others—they are to reflect what it means to be a Christian. Since we live as members of a community, it is not surprising that all three practices are ways of improving our relationships with others, with God, and with ourselves.

Almsgiving is a way of sharing with others our gifts and resources, be they material or spiritual, and thus acknowledging the value of the other person. Prayer, which is dialogue with God, deepens our experience of God's presence, strengthens our knowledge of God, and makes us more aware of our dependence on the one who created us and sustains us in life. Fasting is one way to become more aware of who we are and what we place at the center of our lives.

The gospel reminds us that Lent is a time to open ourselves to conversion, to a change of heart that brings greater life to us as individuals and to our community. **SR. BARBARA A. BOZAK, CSJ**

Responding *to the* Word

Joel wants us to change on the inside and not just externally. *What change of attitude do I most want to make this Lent?*

Final Thoughts...

1ST SUNDAY *of* LENT

Years ago I was traveling across India on a train that ran along a high embankment. The region was flooded, and water stretched as far as the eye could see. Hilltop villages had become islands, and people lined the railway track, begging to get on and get away to safety. A man got in our carriage carrying a sack of potatoes and holding his small daughter by the hand. It was all he had managed to save.

With climate change, floods, droughts, and famines will become more and more common. The environmental crisis tempts us to despair, but Jesus shows the way in the wilderness.

The devil faced Jesus with three familiar temptations: to use his power to be materially secure (never hungry), physically safe (comfortable), and politically successful (in control). Wealth, comfort, and political power are the motors that drive climate change. They are normal human impulses, and Jesus is also human—but he rejects them. He does this by repeatedly turning to God and God's word. He centers himself in another kind of power, far greater and more mysterious than what the devil offers. It is the power of love. This is the power that will save us, ultimately, from destroying ourselves.

This Lent, Jesus asks us to "give up" acquiring more stuff, and "give up" seeking comfort and control so we can experience his kind of power. We're all on this train together.

LOUISE BLAIR

PEOPLE AND PRAYERS TO REMEMBER THIS WEEK

Responding *to the* Word

In Genesis, God provides everything that the human couple needs. *How can I give thanks for all the gifts God has given to me?*

READINGS OF THE DAY

Genesis 2.7-9, 16-18, 25; 3.1-7

Psalm 51

Romans 5.12-19

Matthew 4.1-11

Final Thoughts...

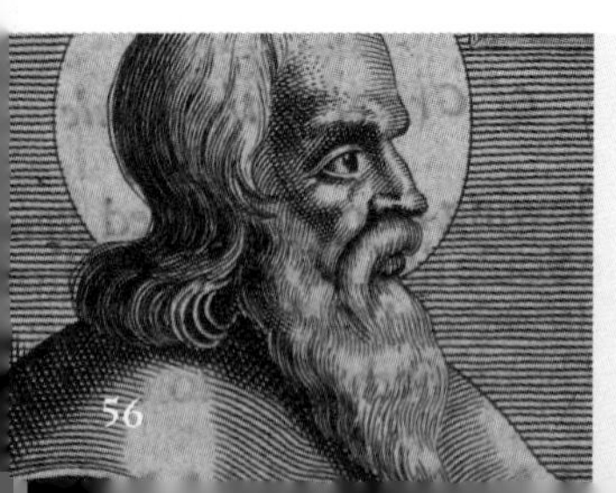

FEASTS THIS WEEK

February 23: **St. Polycarp**
February 27: **St. Gregory of Narek**

2ND SUNDAY *of* **LENT**

Change is hard; we fear it, we resist it, we deny it. Whether we are sent, summoned, or called to accompany someone, we are often reluctant to strike out on a new and unfamiliar path. We take comfort in the familiar, even if it is sometimes difficult. "Better the devil you know," runs the refrain we tell ourselves.

But as much as we resist, change is a part of life. We grow from infant to child to adult. We move away from our parents; we find new partners. We get sick, we grow old, we die—the same happens to all of us.

"Go from your country and your kindred and your father's house to the land that I will show you" is a frightening command—but Abram obeys. He becomes a nomad, traveling far and enduring much, but in the end he is rewarded with the destiny promised him, becoming the father of the Chosen People.

And so it is with us; we face change, much of it hard—whether we like it or not. But it is in the hard times especially that we grow, that we become transformed. Sometimes change is a gradual process: in setting aside time for quiet reflection on the meaning of our lives in faith, we become aware of the crucible in which our faith is refined and purified. Lent offers us such an opportunity. **PATRICK DOYLE**

Responding *to the* Word

Abram gave up much to do as the Lord commanded. ***What must I give up this Lent to let God take up more space in my life?***

READINGS OF THE DAY

Genesis 12.1-4

Psalm 33

2 Timothy 1.8b-10

Matthew 17.1-9

Final Thoughts...

3RD SUNDAY *of* LENT

Having been in the Nevada desert in 106 °F weather, I can understand how thirst can overwhelm and can even lead to death.

In John's gospel we encounter a Samaritan woman preparing to draw water from a well during the hottest time of the day. This daily, ordinary ritual becomes an extraordinary, transformative life experience for her. At the well she encounters one not bound by the legalism of religious authorities, but instead by the law of love written on his heart by God who led him to her. As a woman, a Samaritan and one married to five men, she was an outcast. Not blinded by categories, imperfections, or sins, Jesus models for us all how to satisfy the deepest human thirsts. This is Jesus the pastoral minister whose words water the human soul.

The Samaritan woman, like all of us, thirsts for understanding and acceptance, which are hard to find in a patriarchal society marked by rigid religious laws. Jesus offers her cleansing water of the truth of her life experience. There is no harsh, judgmental rebuke. This truthful encounter is tempered by loving acceptance.

We all thirst for meaning in life. Our faith needs watering. Jesus encounters each of us at the well of our lives and offers unconditional love. With all catechumens preparing for baptism, let us join the entire community in answering Jesus' renewed invitation to selfless service.

SR. JUDY MORRIS, OP

Responding *to the* Word

The Samaritan woman grows in her knowledge of Jesus through her conversation with him. *How can I increase my time in prayer and conversation with Jesus this Lent?*

READINGS OF THE DAY

Exodus 17.3-7

Psalm 95

Romans 5.1-2, 5-8

John 4.5-42

Final Thoughts...

FEASTS THIS WEEK

March 9: **St. Frances of Rome**

4TH SUNDAY *of* LENT

The Lenten Scriptures introduce us to some of the most intriguing people in the Bible. Today we meet David the anointed one and the man born blind. Both experienced God's extraordinary action—a power that took them out of their ordinary lives and drew them into the kingdom work of proclaiming God's marvelous deeds.

In a few short weeks, those who are now preparing for baptism will come to the Easter Vigil in response to the call we hear in today's epistle: "Sleeper awake! Rise from the dead, and Christ will shine on you." These people are experiencing God's extraordinary action in their lives, and they are coming to understand this action in the heart of the Christian community.

Today many parishes are celebrating the Second Scrutiny, a precious gift to those preparing for baptism and to all of us who share in this Sunday Eucharist. We ask God to give the elect the grace and the power to look carefully at their own lives in the light of God's purpose, to recognize what needs to be taken away or changed, and to iden-tify what can be strengthened in God's grace. We also ask for the grace of continuing conver-sion, for each and every one of us. This is the work of Lent, a work that brings light to us all.

MARILYN SWEET

Responding *to the* Word

God looks beyond the appearances into the heart of each person. *How can I get beyond the appearances when meeting and dealing with others?*

Final Thoughts...

FEASTS THIS WEEK

March 17: **St. Patrick**

March 18: **St. Cyril of Jerusalem**

March 19: **St. Joseph**

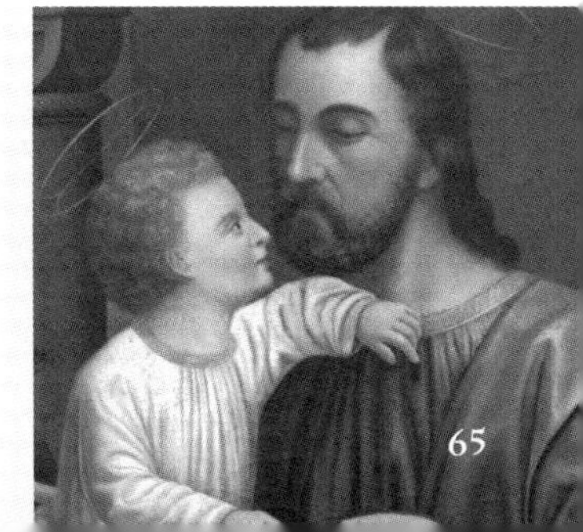

5TH SUNDAY *of* **LENT**

Dear God, so far today, I haven't complained, been selfish, or argued with anyone. But I'm going to get up now, and I'm probably going to need a lot of help. We smile, perhaps recognizing that without God's life-giving Spirit we can become bound in negativity, binding others as well.

The psalmist calls us to hope in God's steadfast love that will not fail to breathe life into us, giving hope and trust. What makes us want to get up in the morning? What gives energy, purpose? Or would we rather hide back under the covers?

Like Martha, we are sometimes overwhelmed by the "stench" of both our own and the world's needs, fearing hope and meaning are impossible. But impossible is not in Jesus' vocabulary. He first expresses gratitude and unwavering trust in God's love. "Father, I thank you for having heard me. I knew that you always hear me." Then Jesus expresses trust in us to give life with the command: "Unbind him." We are to give to others new hope of freedom from whatever imprisons them.

Acknowledging our need and trusting in God's help is a good place to start. With a grateful heart we respond to others in a more compassionate and meaningful way, finding concrete means of helping to "unbind" others in desperate need of new life.

SHERIE RUSLER CROFT

Responding *to the* Word

God promises new life through the
Holy Spirit. *What new spiritual
life have I felt this Lent?*

Final Thoughts...

FEASTS THIS WEEK

March 23: **St. Turibius of Mogrovejo**

March 25: **The Annunciation of the Lord**

PASSION (PALM) SUNDAY

"Let the same mind be in you that was in Christ Jesus," says Paul today, the final Sunday of Lent. The last Sunday—already? Remember Ash Wednesday? All those promises and good intentions! How well have we done? Have our prayer, fasting, and almsgiving borne fruit? "Let the same mind be in you that was in Christ Jesus." This is what our Lenten journey has been about.

What kind of mind did Jesus have? Isaiah, the psalmist, Paul, and Matthew offer us vivid pictures of the mind of Christ. What is striking throughout them all is that Christ rejected the role of helpless victim. He was determined to complete his mission. Listen to the words of Jesus in today's gospel passage. Does he not sound like a man in charge: giving orders right and left, teaching right up to the last? We cannot pity such a man; we stand with him in solidarity, trust, and hope.

Forward he went, trusting that his loving Father would see him through it all. Jesus' steadfast prayer nourished and sustained him. We too have prayed our way to this day. Jesus could do what God asked of him because he had let go of everything, had emptied himself. Letting go is what our prayer, fasting, and almsgiving have been all about. And so today we stand emptied at the table of Lord to be nourished by Christ's body and blood
and filled with the Spirit.

MARGARET BICK

Responding *to the* Word

God's servants endure much for God's sake.
*What suffering has been most
challenging for me to accept recently?*

Final Thoughts...

MASS *of the* LORD'S SUPPER
(HOLY THURSDAY)

On that first Holy Thursday, a profound sacredness accompanied every gesture of Jesus. After sharing his last supper with his friends, Jesus humbly removed his outer garments and, taking up a basin of water and a towel, he began to wash the feet of his disciples. They were all caught by surprise. No master was expected to wash his disciples' feet. When Peter objected, Jesus challenged him: "Unless I wash you, you have no share with me."

In surrendering to Jesus, Peter was showing us how we too must live out our discipleship with Christ. Only by being totally united with him are we able to faithfully serve his mission. With him we will always have hope, whatever trials or suffering we may have to face.

Even as he was about to be handed over to his passion and death, Jesus never stopped loving his disciples, even when out of fear they would temporarily abandon him. We too receive that same love today as we struggle to live our faith. With one humble gesture, washing the feet of his disciples, Jesus has shown us how to be Eucharist, making his presence alive and real in a world that hungers for God's compassion, justice, and peace. Our vocation as his present-day disciples is truly a revolutionary commitment to the life of the world.

REV. MICHAEL TRAHER, SFM

Responding *to the* Word

Jesus gives himself and his life in service of others. ***What can I do to be of greater service for those who are poor and in need?***

CELEBRATION *of the* PASSION *of the* LORD
(GOOD FRIDAY)

It's not about the details of the story. It's not about the garden or the soldiers or the way they divided up his clothes. It's not about Peter or Pontius Pilate or those who watched his death on the cross. It's all about how Jesus took upon himself the fullness of the sorrow and suffering of humanity. And what does that sorrow and suffering look like?

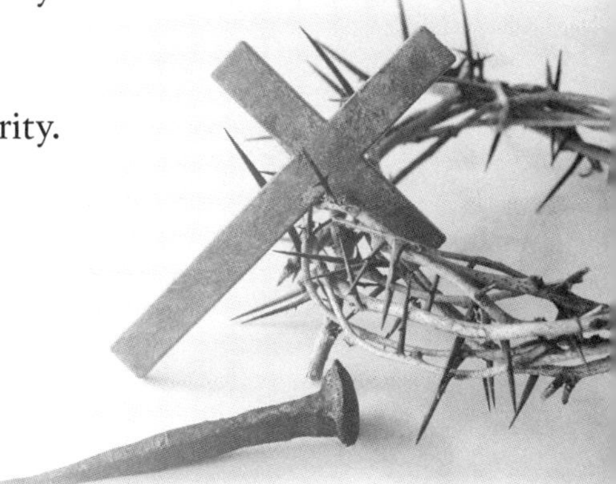

Betrayed by an ally. Abandoned by a friend.
Denounced by his community.
Shouted at by crowds.
Passed from authority to authority.
Physically abused.
Mocked and humiliated.
Misunderstood.
Labelled. Mislabelled.
Stripped of his clothes.
Stripped of his dignity.
Tortured. Executed.

In John's passion, we see reflected the daily experiences of people in our community and around the world. It's not just a story about Jesus. It is a story about all of us. For God so loved the world that he gave his only Son... **SUSAN EATON**

Responding *to the* Word

John's passion story traces Jesus' victory over sin and death. ***Which event in today's gospel was most important to me?***

Final Thoughts...

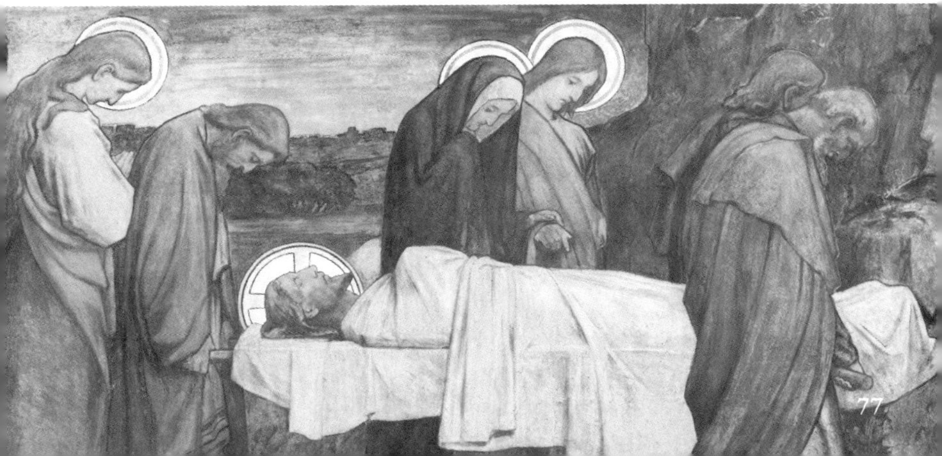

RESURRECTION *of the* LORD
(EASTER VIGIL)

As we begin tonight's Easter Vigil liturgy, our hearts are stirred by the lighting of the new fire, and by having our candles lit to symbolize the risen Christ, Light of the world. The singing of the Exsultet lifts our spirits, and we cherish hearing again the stories of our origins and ancestors in faith.

Tonight's gospel invites us to go with the two Marys, so anxious to visit the tomb where Jesus is buried. Who would have expected that they would encounter an earthquake, the tomb stone rolled back, and angels appearing to say, "He is not here; he has been raised!"? In fear and joy they run to tell the disciples, when suddenly they meet Jesus. Overwhelmed, they embrace his feet and worship him, their hearts telling them something wondrously new is happening.

Easter is not about passively contemplating an empty tomb. It's an invitation to encounter the risen Christ, to believe, to rejoice, and to share the good news. By his resurrection, Jesus reaches out to all who are entombed in the world, setting every heart free from sin and death to embrace his gift of new life.

Tonight, in faith and hope, let us renew our baptismal promises to the risen Lord, in whom death is no more; life is eternal. Let us celebrate in joy his spirit of love among us, transforming all humanity—indeed creation itself. **REV. MICHAEL TRAHER, SFM**

Responding *to the* **Word**

The seven Old Testament readings tell the story of God's saving presence in our world. ***Which reading was I most drawn to tonight? Why?***

Final Thoughts...

RESURRECTION *of the* LORD
(EASTER SUNDAY)

Christian churches around the world resound today with loud and cheerful alleluias to proclaim the greatest good news ever told in human history: Christ has risen from the dead! What makes our joy still greater is that, as St. Paul puts it, we are "raised with Christ." His resurrection opens up forever the future of humankind and of creation. Both our present and our future shine from the radiant light of Christ's victory over death.

Such radiant light first illuminated the women who went to Jesus' tomb after the Sabbath and saw that the stone had been rolled away. At that very tomb, Mary Magdalene had an encounter with the risen Lord. On the same day, the apostles were blessed when Jesus appeared to them, comforting them with the gift of peace and commissioning them to proclaim to the world the good news of his resurrection.

As we celebrate this Eucharist, the risen Lord is in our midst. The paschal candle lit on this very day stands as a reminder of how the resurrection of Christ enlightens every moment and every aspect of our lives. Like Mary Magdalene and the apostles, we, too, are commissioned to share the light, the peace, and the joy that the resurrection of Christ has brought to our own lives. Let us sing—and bring other people to sing along with us—heartfelt and heart-filling alleluias.

 **JEAN-PIERRE PRÉVOST**

Responding *to the* Word

The risen Christ sends us out to be his witnesses. ***What witness to Jesus' words and acts can I give today?***

READINGS
OF THE DAY

Acts 10.34a, 37-43

Psalm 118

**Colossians 3.1-4
or 1 Corinthians
5.6b-8**

**John 20.1-18 or
Matthew 28.1-10**
(Vigil) **or
Luke 24.13-35**
(afternoon Mass)

Final Thoughts...

2ND SUNDAY *of* EASTER
Divine Mercy Sunday

The apostles and disciples of Christ, through their preaching, table-fellowship, and prayers, passed on to others their faith and trust in God's plan of salvation. The readings this Sunday indicate that if we, like the apostles and disciples, live charitably and selflessly, we too can enter the kingdom of heaven. Central to this are the elements of faith and trust.

Just as it was difficult for the apostle Thomas to believe in a resurrected Christ without seeing him and touching him, so too it may be difficult for us at times to believe in heaven or in the plan of salvation. It was the same for the early Christians, as it is for us today: faith is an act of will. Faith is the result of our resolve that we are going to continue to believe in God in a spirit of trust. If we lose this trust, we will be left hopeless and sad. Today's readings urge us to be generous people who exude loving and joyful dispositions that are indicative of our faith and trust in God.

Let us be mindful this week that we too are called to be disciples of Christ with the important mandate to spread the good news of God's plan of salvation. The starting point for us is our conviction that through our belief we will have life—life to the full.

CAROLINE NOLAN

Responding *to the* Word

God's mercy or compassion offers us new life.
How can my compassion for others give them new life?

Final Thoughts...

FEASTS THIS WEEK

April 13: **St. Martin I**

3RD SUNDAY *of* EASTER

How often have we heard the expression "hindsight is 20/20"? In the immediacy of the moment, our vision can be impaired by a lack of information. Today's gospel presents such a situation.

Two disciples meet a stranger on their way to Emmaus and begin updating him on recent events. And what events they are: a prophet, a crucifixion, a missing body, angels. The stranger rebuffs them for their lack of vision and monopolizes the rest of the eleven kilometer walk with a treatise beginning with Moses and ending with Jesus, complete with scriptural references and two thousand years of prophecy.

Being disciples, they are hospitable and, on their arrival in Emmaus, they encourage the stranger to stay the night. He takes them up on their offer, and blesses and breaks bread with them—a pivotal event through which the two disciples will re-interpret their walk with the stranger.

For he is no longer a stranger. He is Jesus! A walk that might have been tedious now becomes heart-burning and miraculous. What was perplexing is now understood.

The two can hardly wait to tell the others. Their tongues rejoice, and in today's liturgy we're still hearing the echoes.

Their hindsight gives us insight into the ordinary events of our lives, into the presence of the Lord in the strangers with whom we walk. Today, may our hearts burn within us! **JOHN WEIR**

Responding *to the* Word

The two disciples found Jesus by understanding the Scriptures and sharing the Eucharist. ***What can I do to discover Christ in these same realities today?***

Final Thoughts...

4TH SUNDAY *of* EASTER
World Day of Prayer for Vocations

In pastoral care, we often refer to "companions on the journey." These are the people who travel with us, particularly through the difficult times when we rely on another person for strength, guidance, and comfort. In Christian life, we model our role of companion for others after Jesus Christ.

In today's readings, Jesus is presented as a shepherd. This imagery reminds us of Jesus' role as companion in our own lives. We know the shepherd as the one who stands between his sheep and all harm. Likewise, we know Jesus as the One who lays down his life for each of us. We know the shepherd as the one who leads the way, choosing the safest path. Likewise, we know Jesus as our guide who directs us on the right path, protecting us with his Spirit. We know the shepherd as the one whose voice his sheep recognize and follow. Likewise, we know Jesus as the one who calls us each by name.

In our hectic lives, when many voices call out and many paths present themselves, and we truly need a companion on the journey, where do we encounter our shepherd? We encounter him today, in this remembrance and celebration of Jesus' sacrifice for us. It is here that our relationship with Jesus is deepened and nurtured. But this is only the beginning. The companion we meet here journeys with us each day, protecting, guiding, and calling us forth by name that we might have life and have it to the fullest.   SHELLEY KUIACK

Responding *to the* Word

Personal conversion and baptism into the community are expected of new followers. ***What changes in my life do I seek during this Easter season?***

Final Thoughts...

FEASTS THIS WEEK

April 28: **St. Peter Chanel**
          St. Louis Grignion de Montfort

April 29: **St. Catherine of Siena**

April 30: **St. Pius V**

May 1: **St. Joseph the Worker**

May 2: **St. Athanasius**

5TH SUNDAY *of* EASTER

A concern brought Rose to the parish social justice committee. Problems had forced the local soup kitchen to cut back. This meant two fewer days of hot meals a week for the hungry. She asked a simple question: could our parish hall and kitchen be used to fill the gap?

Where would we find the needed volunteers? Who would provide the food and cover unforeseen costs? Finally, the parish agreed to take on a weekend soup kitchen as a temporary Lenten project.

Some twenty years—and many thousands of meals—later, this ecumenical effort continues to answer a basic community need. But what if the concern brought to that committee had been on human trafficking in a far-off land or an industrial project threatening the environment and traditional lifestyles? How would we have responded?

Luke tells us in Acts how the early Christian community reacted to a social concern that crossed ethnic and class lines. They took on the task of caring for widows while not neglecting the word of God, and "the number of the disciples increased greatly."

As individuals, we cannot respond to every issue. However, as Peter says in the second reading, "Like living stones, let yourselves be built into a spiritual house." All of us have our own roles to play in building a Christian community, which knows Jesus is "the way, and the truth and the life."

MICHAEL DOUGHERTY

Responding *to the* Word

The Twelve call others to service in the community. ***What new service can I offer to my community?***

Final Thoughts...

6TH SUNDAY *of* EASTER

In these weeks after Easter we are making our way through the Book of Acts. Its title is the Acts of the Apostles but we should really read it as the Acts of the Holy Spirit, continuing the work of Christ and enabling his disciples to become like Christ. We see them preaching like Christ and working miracles like his. In today's reading we see them being persecuted by the same people who crucified Christ and, just as the cross gives the gospel its power, so the persecution of the apostles spreads the good news around the world.

In Samaria, Peter and John bestow the Spirit upon those who have been baptized into Christ. They have the power to do this because Christ has already bestowed the Spirit on them. John's gospel repeatedly emphasizes that Christ's first and greatest gift is the gift of the Spirit, the Paraclete, who acts as our advocate and speaks through and for us. The Paraclete, the Advocate, is thus the Spirit of truth who leads believers into all truth. The Spirit dwells within our hearts, for the Spirit is love who unites us with the Father in Christ. Next Sunday we will celebrate the Lord's Ascension. We should not think of the Spirit as a poor replacement for Christ, but rather as God uniting us with Christ who lives in glory in the union of the Father. It is the glorification of Christ that we celebrate in this Eucharist by the power of the Spirit.

JENNIFER COOPER

Responding *to the* Word

The crowds respond with joy to the words and signs that reveal Christ. ***What has caused me to rejoice during this Easter season?***

Final Thoughts...

FEASTS THIS WEEK

May 12: **St. Nereus & St. Achilleus**
St. Pancras

May 13: **Our Lady of Fatima**

May 14: **St. Matthias**
The Ascension of the Lord
(in some dioceses of the USA)

May 15: **St. Isidore**

THE ASCENSION *of the* **LORD**
World Communication Day

Matthew's telling of the Ascension story is both ironic and comforting. The twelve apostles are central figures in his gospel, which is directed to a community steeped in Jewish tradition. They are sent out to inspire, to teach, and to lead in the renewal of the twelve tribes of Israel. After the tragedy of Judas' betrayal and suicide, there are only eleven of them. Now known as disciples (learners) rather than apostles (messengers), they continue to learn what discipleship means.

Jesus does not call the eleven to the Temple Mount in Jerusalem, the seat of Israel's tradition and hope. Instead, he summons them to an anonymous mountain in Galilee. Seeing him there, they worship, but doubt. Worship and doubt don't logically go together, but even for us today they coexist as elements of a genuine personal faith.

When Jesus approaches, he does not scold them or try to argue away their doubts. Instead, he offers a stirring invitation to move forward, to include the whole world in their circle of worship and doubt, to make disciples of all nations.

As with Christians of any generation, the eleven disciples' struggles would become their greatest asset in reaching out to men and women of every imaginable background and way of life. Because they knew for themselves both worship and doubt, they, like so many after them, were credible witnesses to Jesus' mysterious presence—even to the end of the age. **REV. CORBIN EDDY**

** The 7th Sunday of Easter is celebrated in some dioceses of the USA today. Refer to p. 102.*

Responding *to the* Word

When Jesus ascends, he promises the Holy Spirit to help us continue his work of bringing others to him. *What can I do to help someone learn about Christ today?*

Final Thoughts...

7TH SUNDAY *of* EASTER

The theme of today's readings takes us to a time and a place in the future. They take us beyond the immediate challenges that we are facing in our life and encourage us to trust in faith.

The psalm speaks of the orphans, the widows, the prisoners, the homeless. Each one is given what he needs: a father for the orphans, a protector for the widow, prosperity to the prisoner, a home for the homeless.

While the struggles we live and the problems we face can often paralyze us in life and prevent us from living fully, today's readings open up a new horizon of possibilities. They stretch what is now and allow us to imagine what can be. We need not be stuck in our current state of struggle. We can overcome. But we need to trust in the profound goodness of God and his ability to transform our life. For God anything is possible.

The season of Easter attests to the biggest miracle of all—God raising the Son from death to life. God's ability to overturn situations of death and bring out new life when all seems lost is what shapes and grows our faith. Nothing is impossible for God. We have to remember and live according to this belief if we wish to see miracles in our lives.

NATALIA KONONENKO

Responding *to the* Word

Jesus offers us an example in the way that he prays for us. *For whom do I wish to pray today?*

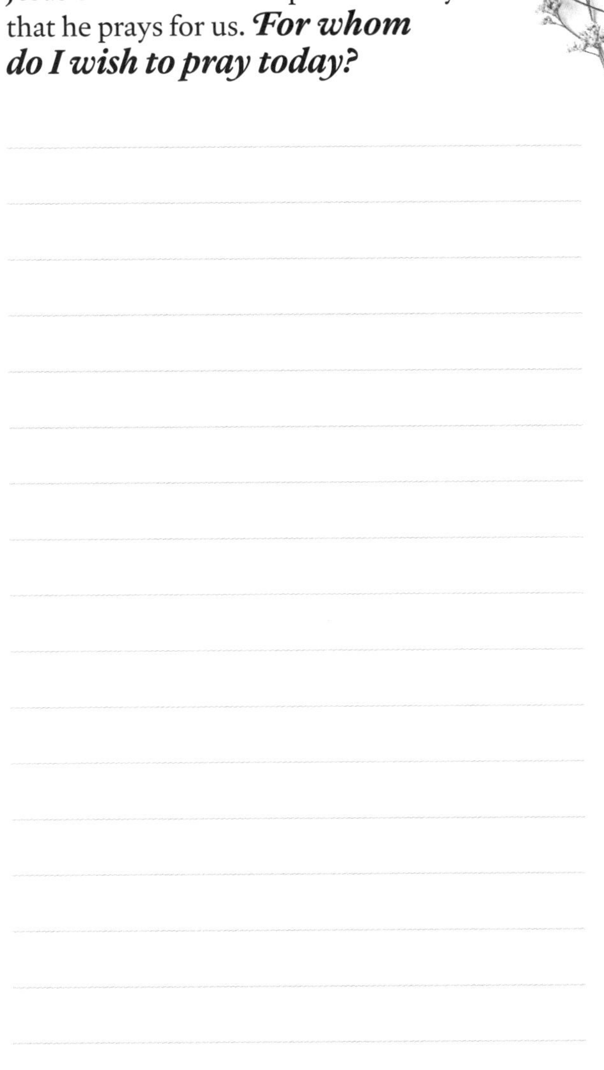

Final Thoughts...

PENTECOST SUNDAY

If you had a singing voice only your mother could love, could you sing a leading role in an opera? If you couldn't run faster than a snail, could you be a member of an Olympic track team?

These examples are exaggerated, but there are times when we are asked to do something for which we feel ourselves entirely unqualified. At the Ascension, the disciples were challenged to take the good news to the whole world. Lest such a task seem beyond their power, Jesus told them to wait until the Spirit came. They waited. The Spirit came. We celebrate that coming today, the feast of Pentecost.

The first reading tells us how the Holy Spirit descended upon Jesus' followers, giving them the power to reach out with the good news to all the nations of the world.

In the second reading, Paul makes clear what the Spirit does for us. First the Spirit enables us to say "Jesus is Lord." Then the gifts of the Holy Spirit inspire all the activities of Christians so that they can accomplish God's purpose for the world.

In the gospel, John adds another dimension to what the Spirit gives us. Through the Spirit the Church possesses the power to forgive sin. We all are to forgive and heal one another. Too often we forget we have this power.

Though we are given the great challenge to bring all peoples to Christ, we cannot do this by ourselves. We can do it only in and through the Spirit. **REV. JOHN SPICER, CSSR**

Responding *to the* Word

The Holy Spirit bestows gifts of service on us to build up the community. *How am I using my spiritual gifts for the benefit of others?*

Final Thoughts...

FEASTS THIS WEEK

May 25: **The Blessed Virgin Mary,
Mother of the Church**

May 26: **St. Philip Neri**

May 27: **St. Augustine of Canterbury**

May 29: **St. Paul VI**

THE MOST HOLY TRINITY

"**G**od so loved the world…" Love is the first step in the dance, and God always takes the lead. It's the dance into which we have been introduced at our baptism: life in the Trinity.

If you want to begin to approach the mystery of the Trinity as anything other than a mathematical equation, begin with love. It's love poured out, love given, love received and shared that is the essence of this mystery. Then, think love in motion—not a static equation, but love moving between persons whom we name as Father, Son, and Spirit. Think of a dance between three equal lovers who have nothing else to do but love. That's the essence of Trinitarian life.

We tend to think of the Trinity as "up there" (or over there)—distant from us (a distance that absolves us from any obligation to participate!). But Trinity, in fact, is our home address. We live in the Trinity. From the time of our baptism, we have been caught up in the dance that is love poured out, handed over, returned, shared. This love is our highest calling, our source of morality and our greatest delight.

That humanity is invited into the communion of love that is the God of Jesus Christ boggles our minds. But don't get caught in the boggle. Ignore your two left feet. Let God lead you in the best dance of your life. **BERNADETTE GASSLEIN**

Responding *to the* Word

Jesus did not come to condemn us but to teach us how to love. ***When am I more ready to condemn than to love? Why?***

READINGS
OF THE DAY

Exodus 34.4b-6, 8-9

Daniel 3

2 Corinthians 13.11-13

John 3.16-18

Final Thoughts...

FEASTS THIS WEEK

June 1: **St. Justin**

June 2: **St. Marcellinus & St. Peter**

June 3: **St. Charles Lwanga & Companions**

June 5: **St. Boniface**

June 6: **St. Norbert**

THE BODY *and* BLOOD *of* CHRIST

The feast of the Body and Blood of Christ is traditionally known as "Corpus Christi." The gospel tells us that Jesus is the "living bread." When we give real bread to the poor, we give nourishment to suffering humanity, the "whole Christ" who hungers for the bread of justice.

Years ago I was at a Mass in the highlands of Peru. After the liturgy, a woman placed a bundle on top of the table used as an altar, and said, "We have just celebrated the Mass of Jesus; now we will celebrate the Mass of the Poor." She unwrapped the bundle and took bread, corn, and yucca and placed them in our hands. "Since we are poor we eat with our fingers as a sign of our solidarity with one another and our struggle for justice." I will never forget the experience of receiving nourishment from the poor.

When we chant the Great Amen at the Eucharist, we affirm in song that we are the body of Christ. Before receiving communion, St. Augustine held the bread before the people and said: "Receive what you are and be what you receive." Once fed with the Eucharist, we renew our commitment to serve Christ in those who hunger and thirst in so many ways for a healthy and dignified life. How can we be food and nourishment to someone who needs a caring presence or listening ear? Today's feast is a rallying cry to service. "Whatever you do to the least of my brothers and sisters, you do it to me."

REV. ROBERT F. DUEWEKE, OSA

Responding *to the* Word

Sharing in the Eucharist brings us into greater communion, both with God and with others. ***What can I do to show my unity with others when I participate in the Eucharist?***

Final Thoughts...

FEASTS THIS WEEK

June 9: **St. Ephrem**

June 11: **St. Barnabas**

June 12: **The Most Sacred Heart of Jesus**

June 13: **St. Anthony of Padua**
The Immaculate Heart of the
Blessed Virgin Mary

11TH SUNDAY *in* ORDINARY TIME

From the very beginning, God has called priests and prophets to listen to God's voice, keep God's covenant, and shepherd God's people. God's love and faithfulness last through every age. This saving grace is freely given, and in Christ we are reconciled with our Creator.

In the gospel we hear of Christ's deep compassion for the people wandering like sheep without a shepherd. His newly appointed disciples have various talents and strengths; they are given authority and power to expel unclean spirits, heal the sick, and raise the dead. They are sent as laborers to help with the harvest and gather the lost sheep, with a reminder that as freely they have received, so freely they are to give.

We too come from all walks of life with various talents and gifts. We have said "yes" to Jesus, "yes" to being disciples and laborers. What is our specific mission, our special calling in our own lives, in our own communities?

In celebration today we give thanks for all that we have been given. We rejoice that by listening, responding, and giving to others we nurture lives and build stronger relationships. Our hearts are touched by Christ's deep compassion, and healing takes place more richly than we fully know. **KELLY ANNE MANTLER**

Responding *to the* Word

The people of the covenant are to be God's "special possession." ***How can I thank God for being included in the new covenant people?***

Final Thoughts...

FEASTS THIS WEEK

June 19: **St. Romuald**

116

12TH SUNDAY *in* ORDINARY TIME

"**B**ut everyone else is doing it!" It's such a common phrase. School kids teasing the loner? Executives padding their expense accounts? Neighbors gossiping about the family down the street? "Everyone else is doing it!" It's easy to just go with the flow, to abdicate responsibility for our own actions.

Deep down inside, we all realize that it doesn't matter what everyone else is doing—what matters is what *we* are doing. As followers of Jesus, we are called to witness to the truth of God's kingdom, regardless of what everyone else does. By doing what is right and just, we acknowledge God who is Lord of all life.

Easy to say, but much more difficult to live out in daily life. Just ask the teenager who defies the bully at school. Or the person who stands up for what is right and risks ridicule, rejection, or worse. Of all people, Jesus knew what can happen when we swim against the tide of popular opinion.

In today's gospel, Jesus promises us that we will never be left alone when we try to do what is right. He doesn't say it will be easy. What he does say is that whenever we speak up for truth and justice, God is on our side, sustaining us and holding us up in difficult and challenging times. Indeed, the Lord is with us! **TERESA WHALEN LUX**

Responding *to the* Word

Jesus' death and resurrection began the overthrow of evil's power in our world. *What can I do today to increase the amount of good and lessen the amount of evil?*

Final Thoughts...

FEASTS THIS WEEK

June 22: **St. Paulinus of Nola**
St. John Fisher & St. Thomas More

June 24: **The Nativity of St. John the Baptist**

June 27: **St. Cyril of Alexandria**

13TH SUNDAY *in* ORDINARY TIME

We are invited this week to reflect once more on the call and meaning of discipleship. Our discipleship is rooted in baptism in the death and resurrection of Jesus Christ. The reading from 2 Kings and our gospel today make concrete a demand of discipleship: namely, hospitality.

Traveling recently, I found myself surrounded by cultures that seemed strange and languages in which I wasn't very fluent. I continue to be grateful for those who offered me hospitality in the form of shelter and food, a friendly smile and conversation, orienting me to the culture and patterns of those around me, introducing me to new friends and colleagues, helping me to understand and be understood.

The unnamed woman of the first reading offers the passerby a meal. She later recognizes Elisha as a "holy" man and again provides him with a space to rest and a meal. Who are the unsung or even unnamed people in my life? Might I offer a prayer or a gesture or a blessing to those persons? Who are the passersby God might be inviting us to welcome? In the gospel, Jesus calls each of us to be rooted in him. We are urged to love and welcome others, to offer even a cup of water, as a disciple of Jesus, recognizing Christ in the family member and in the stranger.

We give thanks and praise today for God's goodness and steadfast love. We pledge ourselves to be women and men, children and youth of gospel hospitality. In this way we live the call to be disciples of Jesus.

SR. CARMEN DISTON, IBVM

Responding *to the* Word

Jesus talks about the radical loyalty required to follow him. ***What (or whom) have I needed to give up in my life to be faithful to Jesus?***

Final Thoughts...

FEASTS THIS WEEK

June 29: **St. Peter & St. Paul**

June 30: **First Martyrs of the Holy Roman Church**

July 1: **St. Junípero Serra**

July 3: **St. Thomas**

July 4: **Independence Day**

14TH SUNDAY *in* ORDINARY TIME

The Lord's Prayer remains an unsurpassed model for all Christian prayers. Jesus taught it to his disciples when they asked him how to pray. But Jesus uttered many other prayers. The one we hear in today's gospel should be just as precious to us. Some have called it "Jesus' Magnificat."

It is indeed a Magnificat, whose main thrust is thanksgiving and praise—thanksgiving and praise still related to God as "Father," but also as the "Lord of heaven and earth." For Jesus, God the Savior, and God the Creator are one God. The beauty of creation and the generosity of the Creator already say something about the beauty and richness of God's salvation. Are we not tempted to forget the inclusion of creation in our prayer?

And this God, Lord of creation, is not an authoritarian God or a God who can be reached only by "the wise and the intelligent." No, the God of Jesus is a humble God, "gentle and humble in heart," a God who is at home in the hearts of the lowly and of those who are left aside or despised. They are the ones dear to his heart. More than that, the God of Jesus cares for them as Jesus does: "Come to me, all you that are weary and are carrying heavy burdens, and I will give you rest." What a beautiful prayer, this Magnificat prayed by Jesus! It tells us who our God really is: the all-powerful Creator, and yet the loving and caring Father of each one of us. **JEAN-PIERRE PRÉVOST**

Responding *to the* Word

Jesus invites us to put our burdens on him.
*What burden do I most want
to give to Jesus today?*

Final Thoughts...

15TH SUNDAY *in* ORDINARY TIME

There are few things in life that give my mother greater reward than tending to her vegetable garden. She knows that the success of her harvest largely begins and ends with the condition of the soil. So each year before planting, she adds the right nutrients and organic matter for strong, healthy roots. Then it's on to the next step to prepare the earth some more.

The relationship that gardeners and farmers have with their land is not all that different from the one that God has with every Christian. We, too, are soil, but for the divine seed. We, too, are plants, dependent on our sower to help us reach healthy maturity.

In today's gospel, Jesus tells us about the seed that was scattered broadcast and fell onto the path, the rocky ground, the thorns. Using this parable, he wants us to understand that God pours out his grace on everyone. All of us are given the help we need for salvation.

No matter what our lives may have been in the past, nothing is ever lost with God. We can still become the "good soil" that bears fruit even though we may have been led astray. What are the prerequisites for getting back on track? There are three of them: a contrite and humble heart, a soul that is prepared to receive the Holy Spirit, and holy stubbornness to persevere in the face of difficulties.

PATRICIA TAKEDA

Responding *to the* Word

God's word changes our world. *What changes have I experienced due to my attention to Scripture?*

Final Thoughts...

FEASTS THIS WEEK

July 13: **St. Henry**
July 14: **St. Kateri Tekakwitha**
July 15: **St. Bonaventure**
July 16: **Our Lady of Mount Carmel**
July 18: **St. Camillus de Lellis**

16TH SUNDAY *in* ORDINARY TIME

Nature provides many metaphors for the kingdom of God. For instance, a garden or a farm usually has desirable plants plus weeds. Similarly, faith communities are made up of imperfect individuals at various stages of spiritual growth. In the first parable in today's gospel, the farmer does not weed his field because that might also damage the good plants. So too God does not "prune" the community of believers, but waits until each person's true nature is revealed. Like the farmer, God knows that things are not always what they first appear to be. God is patient, allowing us time to mature, recognizing that something that initially looks undesirable might turn out to be something very good.

The parables of the mustard seed and the leaven show that something quite small can have a very large effect. The tiniest seed grows into a large tree, while a small bit of yeast leavens an entire batch of flour. Thus, those who think God is only in magnificent buildings, major events, or important people may be blind to God's activity in and through what appears to be less significant. But some of the greatest saints had humble beginnings and spent their lives doing "little" things. We need to be open to the next Francis of Assisi, Thérèse of Lisieux, or Mother Teresa. The kingdom of heaven really is like a mustard seed or a pinch of yeast.

JOHN L. MCLAUGHLIN

Responding *to the* Word

Jesus tells us that God's presence (kingdom) often starts out very small but can grow very large. *How has my awareness of God grown recently?*

Final Thoughts...

131

17TH SUNDAY *in* ORDINARY TIME
World Day for Grandparents & the Elderly

"What will you give me?" is the question many of us ask when we sign up for the reward points some businesses offer. We feel in control as we feverishly collect the points for yet more travel, a new gadget, extra points to buy more.

In today's first reading, we may be puzzled by God's question to Solomon. "Ask what I should give you." From our vantage point, we think of all the things he could have asked for. Solomon's response of "an understanding mind" takes us somewhat off-guard. His surprising response invites us to look at the treasure hidden in the field of our acquisitive consumerism. God's response to Solomon, as he grants his request, reiterates the importance of going deeper. And Jesus himself said, "Where your treasure is, there your heart is also."

The parable stories in the gospel invite us to see the reign of God as that treasure. In the reign of right relationships, it takes a wise and understanding heart to truly link our deepest longings with justice, justice for all, an eco-justice in an interdependent and interconnected universe. Such justice is about learning how to live more simply, so others can simply live. The parables detail this journey into our deepest longings. At the end of these parables, Jesus' probing question is all about finding that treasure deep within and, having found it, living up to what it demands in our individual lives. He asks afresh, "Have you understood all this?" **SR. JANET MALONE, CND**

Responding *to the* Word

Solomon asks God for an understanding heart.
What would I ask God for?

Final Thoughts...

FEASTS THIS WEEK

July 29: **St. Martha, St. Mary, & St. Lazarus**
July 30: **St. John Chrysologus**
July 31: **St. Ignatius of Loyola**
August 1: **St. Alphonsus Liguori**

18TH SUNDAY *in* ORDINARY TIME

It's barbecue season, time for good food and refreshing drink. If we're sharing a meal with friends, we make sure that there's plenty to go around: if we don't have leftovers, then maybe someone didn't get enough to eat! And if it's a scorcher, we need a steady supply of cool beverages to keep pace with everyone's thirst.

Do you ever think of the miracle of the loaves and fish when preparing for a party? Do you think of the Eucharist when you have unexpected guests? Food and drink are the core elements of our eucharistic gathering, and Jesus' miracle in today's gospel offers a key insight into the mystery of sharing what we have with others.

The disciples saw disaster looming, but they were relying on what little they could find themselves. Jesus brings the crowd together with a blessing, and there is miraculous abundance. Generosity, open giving, true community ensure that there will be leftovers.

When we gather for the Eucharist, we bring our gifts: bread, wine, monetary offerings. We might also bring our voices in song, our leadership in ministry. And we bring our pain, our need, our brokenness. Isaiah writes, "Come to me; listen, so that you may live." Our Eucharist—our life—is complete when we share all we have and are, making sure that everyone can eat and be filled—with leftovers to spare! **NANCY KEYES**

Responding *to the* Word

When the disciples cannot feed the crowd, Jesus takes their food and does. *What "food" can I offer so that others can be nourished today?*

Final Thoughts...

August 4: **St. John Vianney**

August 5: **Dedication of the Basilica of St. Mary Major**

August 6: **The Transfiguration of the Lord**

August 7: **St. Sixtus II & Companions St. Cajetan**

August 8: **St. Dominic**

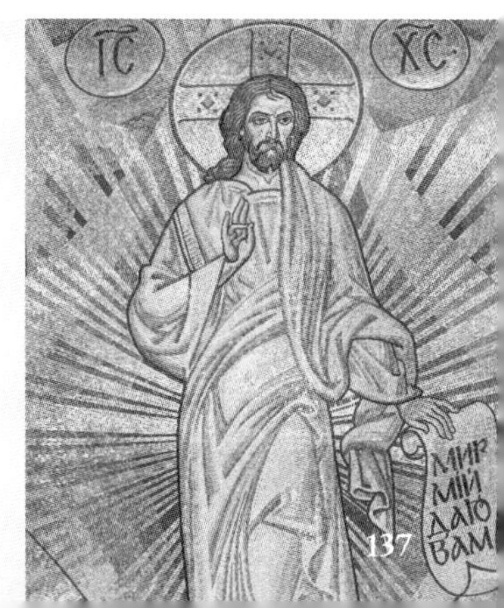

19TH SUNDAY *in* **ORDINARY TIME**

What if Peter had listened the first time? "Take heart, it is I; do not be afraid," Jesus told him when Peter became fearful at seeing Christ walk on water. Why did Peter have to ask for proof? And why such dramatic proof?

Peter was quite bold in making demands of Jesus. How different might the story have been if Peter had calmed down, sat back, and waited for Jesus to reach the boat. On the surface, not much would have changed. The wind would have ceased, and the disciples would still have that revelation of the reality of Jesus.

Most paintings of this scene show a stern, commanding Jesus on the water. However, by now Jesus must have known what to expect from Peter. Perhaps a knowing, loving grin might be more appropriate for these portraits. That's how I like to imagine Christ when I finally realize the truth of a situation. Like Peter, I take a lot of convincing, especially when God is involved. We long for instant solutions and dramatic signs. We are all Peter.

If Peter had thought a moment, he might have taken a lesson from Elijah, who waited for the silence. We're not good at silence. And we're not good at listening, especially listening to God. Perhaps we all need to pray often the first verse of today's psalm, "Let me hear what God the Lord will speak." **MARGARET BICK**

Responding *to the* Word

Elijah hears God only in the faint, whispering sound. ***What tiny whispers from God have I noticed recently?***

Final Thoughts...

FEASTS THIS WEEK

August 10: **St. Lawrence**

August 11: **St. Clare**

August 12: **St. Jane Frances de Chantal**

August 13: **St. Pontian & St. Hippolytus**

August 14: **St. Maximilian Kolbe**

August 15: **The Assumption of the Blessed Virgin Mary**

THE ASSUMPTION *of the* BLESSED VIRGIN MARY

Mary's prayer in today's gospel passage is both humble and confident. Following her cousin Elizabeth's proclamation of Mary as blessed among women, Mary replies with her hymn of praise to God: her Magnificat.

Mary says, "My soul magnifies the Lord" and firmly sets her confidence in God. Though birthing God for the world must have seemed utterly impossible to Mary, she trusts that God will fulfill God's plans with her. Her ongoing faith-filled response to God's call, uniquely miraculous and difficult as it is, should inspire us to trust in God with such radical confidence ourselves—not a confidence that overinflates our sense of self, elevating ourselves above others, but one that is rooted in God's care and mercy. This value on humble confidence is echoed later: God "has brought down the powerful...and lifted up the lowly." Though Jesus has not yet been born, Mary recognizes that God is already present in the midst of God's people in a new way in her pregnant body, to which John responds with joy while still in Elizabeth's womb.

Mary carries Jesus in her womb; we carry him with our lives. May we see that God invites us to embrace the humble confidence of Mary in our own lives, recognizing that God is already at work in us to bring mercy into the world.

KELLY BOURKE

Responding *to the* Word

Mary's song of praise speaks of God lifting up the lowly. ***Where have I seen God bring about justice in an unjust situation?***

Final Thoughts...

20TH SUNDAY *in* ORDINARY TIME

My mother used to tell me to be nice to everyone in school and to help them if needed, "even if you don't feel like it."

Today's gospel about the woman from Canaan is a demonstration of God's kindness. It also highlights the virtues of faith, humility, and perseverance. When Jesus did not heed her request the first time, and his disciples urged him to ignore her, the Canaanite woman fell to her knees and humbled herself before him. Moved by her faith, Jesus cured her daughter. There was something about her faith and humility and her unwillingness to get discouraged that impressed Jesus. She believed in him, and she came out of that encounter refreshed and renewed.

Jesus' mercy and justice shine through in this encounter. We can imitate his example and open our hearts to all people, no matter where they come from, no matter what the difficulties are. For it is only through this openness of spirit that we communicate and share with everyone the essence of God's love. Reverend Richard Humke, an Episcopalian priest, noted: "In the context of the Lord's supper, where we all come knowing that none of us is perfect and that each of us has failed…something good happens in our life as a community when we notice the people around us." Jesus noticed the woman from Canaan for her faith. "Woman, great is your faith!"

He invites us to open our hearts and believe. **SHARON QUEANO**

Responding *to the* Word

The persistent woman will accept no excuse from Jesus about why he will not heal her daughter. ***For what am I continually asking Jesus in my prayer?***

Final Thoughts...

FEASTS THIS WEEK

August 19: **St. John Eudes**

August 20: **St. Bernard**

August 21: **St. Pius X**

August 22: **The Queenship of the Blessed Virgin Mary**

21ST SUNDAY *in* ORDINARY TIME

How often have we heard the old adage: practice makes perfect. It drove me crazy when Mom would say it as I practiced my piano scales yet again. But Peter's declaration of faith in today's gospel is a good case in point of just how true that saying really is. Throughout the gospels, we see the many times Peter tried to practice his faith in Jesus. Attempting to walk on water—and sinking! Or swearing that he will stand by Jesus—and then denying him!

And yet, today's gospel is a shining example of a time when Peter did get it right, when all of his practice finally paid off. Out of all Jesus' followers, Peter is the one whose faith allows him to be the first to proclaim that Jesus is the Messiah.

Each week when we come together to celebrate the Eucharist, we, too, profess our faith in Jesus as God's only Son, our Lord. And each week we are sent forth to practice—and to put into practice—what we have proclaimed. When we refuse to hold on to hurts or grudges and offer forgiveness to another, when we welcome the newly arrived refugee next door, when we act with compassion to the less fortunate, we practice what we have proclaimed.

"Who do you say that I am?" Today, we go forth to live out the answer in the world. **TERESA WHALEN LUX**

Responding *to the* Word

God's doorkeeper must not abuse their authority but care for those under their authority. ***How might I care more for those under my authority?***

Final Thoughts...

August 24: **St. Bartholomew**

August 25: **St. Louis**
        St. Joseph Calasanz

August 27: **St. Monica**

August 28: **St. Augustine**

August 29: **The Passion of St. John the Baptist**

22ND SUNDAY *in* ORDINARY TIME

Peter's lack of comprehension in this gospel passage should be a source of comfort and encouragement for modern Christians. If Peter, who lived with Jesus daily, could misunderstand Jesus, then surely there is hope for those of us two thousand years later.

The problem for Peter was that Jesus was not living up to his expectations. The Jews of his time expected the Messiah to be a worldly military leader who would drive the occupying Romans out of Israel. Instead, Jesus talks about going to Jerusalem to be killed. No wonder Peter tries to talk him out of this crazy notion. Peter was unable to go beyond his contemporaries' views and comprehend the radically different thing God was doing through Jesus. Jesus was going to set them free, just not in the way they expected.

We have the benefit of reading this passage in light of the Resurrection, which demonstrated Jesus' power over not just the Romans but over death itself. We know today, in a way Peter could never understand at the time, that by giving up his life in service to others, Jesus would save us. We also know we must do the same if we seek to follow him. Only in giving up our lives in service to others will we have true life, both in this world and in the kingdom of God that is to come. **JOHN L. MCLAUGHLIN**

Responding *to the* Word

Jesus tells us that we must take up our cross and follow him. ***What cross do I most want not to carry in my life now?***

Final Thoughts...

FEASTS THIS WEEK

September 3: **St. Gregory the Great**
September 5: **St. Teresa of Calcutta**

23RD SUNDAY *in* ORDINARY TIME

Today's readings suggest something about the difficulties of building and sustaining community. We all belong to various communities—our family, our classroom or workplace, our parish, our neighborhood—and we know how easily conflicts can arise. Within the life of a community there are frequently disagreements or resentment. We may have to find the courage to speak up when problems arise. Sometimes members of the group may need gentle correction or even firm discipline. "Love your neighbor" is simple enough to say but very difficult to live! There are times when we may wonder whether harmonious human community is even possible.

If we can keep an open and listening heart, as today's psalm advises, we will be better able to discern the voice of God in the midst of our messy efforts to live and work together. In the gospel, Jesus assures us that he is with us in even the smallest gathering "in my name." While we usually interpret this as referring to gatherings for prayer or worship, our faith tells us that God is present among us in every circumstance of our lives.

Living in our various communities will never be easy. Let us pray for the grace to discern God's presence at the heart of those communities, encouraging and supporting us in our struggles to love our neighbor as ourself.

 **KRYSTYNA HIGGINS**

Responding *to the* Word

Jesus encourages us to find a practical way toward reconciliation. ***With whom might I need to reconcile today?***

READINGS OF THE DAY

Ezekiel 33.7-9

Psalm 95

Romans 13.8-10

Matthew 18.15-20

Final Thoughts...

FEASTS THIS WEEK

September 8: **The Nativity of the Blessed Virgin Mary**

September 9: **St. Peter Claver**

September 12: **The Most Holy Name of Mary**

24TH SUNDAY *in* ORDINARY TIME

What a puzzle a human being is! Take that slave in today's gospel passage. His debt was enormous. The king was entitled to balance his books by selling the slave, his few possessions, and even his wife and children—possibly to different owners. But the slave asked for patience on the part of the king and was granted mercy in abundance. The king erased his entire debt! This was beyond what the slave had hoped or asked for. His money problems were gone in an instant.

You'd think this slave would be overflowing with "the milk of human kindness." But no! He had his neighbor thrown into debtors' prison. Truly, this slave's behavior does not make sense. Sin seldom makes sense. We're led to ask, "What were you thinking?!" When we take time to reflect on our own bad acts, we realize that we should have known better; we do know better. This is the mystery of sin.

The king's behavior doesn't make sense either. Who in their right mind would simply erase such a large debt? Who could be so gracious? Who but God, the true king! God's grace is also a mystery. As we leave the liturgy today, we are sent forth in the peace of Christ, carrying within us God's mercy and forgiveness which are meant to be passed on to those we meet this week. **MARGARET BICK**

Responding *to the* Word

Jesus emptied himself to become filled with God's life. *Of what must I empty myself today so that God can live more fully in me?*

____

____

____

____

____

____

Final Thoughts...

____

____

____

____

FEASTS THIS WEEK

September 14: **The Exaltation of the Holy Cross**

September 15: **Our Lady of Sorrows**

September 16: **St. Cornelius & St. Cyprian**

September 17: **St. Hildegard of Bingen
St. Robert Bellarmine**

September 19: **St. Januarius**

25TH SUNDAY *in* ORDINARY TIME

Labor exchanges are one of the more visible locations in our world where the unemployed wait each day, hoping to be offered work. If you have ever been out of work yourself, you will know the feelings of unworthiness and worry the workers in today's gospel experienced. Who would ever hire them again? How would they support their families? Could they survive? The more the day passed, the more desperate they would become.

Today's gospel passage makes it clear these laborers are not lazy. They go to work even at the eleventh hour, having no concrete wage agreement. Imagine their joy, then, and their experience of liberation, when they are given exactly what they need: not "minimum" wage, but a "living" wage that will provide a day's subsistence for each family.

Now imagine we are speaking about salvation instead of employment. For what can we hope? Because our God is gracious and merciful, slow to anger and abounding in steadfast love, good to all and compassionate, we know we are not disadvantaged by coming to faith later rather than earlier, by being regular disciples instead of "The Twelve," by feeling less deserving of God's grace than we perceive our neighbor to be. In thanks, then, we give ourselves over to loving union with Christ, who has revealed and offered freely God's boundless ways of love for all humankind. **CHRISTINE MADER**

Responding *to the* Word

Paul encourages us to conduct ourselves in a way worthy of the gospel. *What can I do today to offer an example of gospel living?*

Final Thoughts...

26TH SUNDAY *in* ORDINARY TIME
World Day of Migrants and Refugees

At a recent meeting we were naming the personal qualities we were looking for in a search to fill an important position. The first quality mentioned was "follow through...she has to have follow through." All of us appreciate those people who actually do what they say they are going to do. We can trust them and depend on them.

In today's gospel Jesus describes two kinds of people—those who say "no" at first but then do it anyhow, and those who say "yes" and don't follow through. In the end, it is those who do God's will who will be judged as righteous. Jesus reminds us that we might be surprised at those we meet in the reign of God. Tax collectors and prostitutes don't seem like likely candidates. What about drug dealers and crooked politicians in our day? How do they line up against the more religious, law-abiding citizens?

As we celebrate the Eucharist, we are a gathering of all kinds of people who are there for all kinds of reasons. It is not for us to judge each other's motivation. What is essential is that all of us are embraced by the unconditional love and mercy of God and by the magnanimity of Jesus whose eternal "yes" liberates us to live in the Spirit.

SR. MARY ELLEN GREEN, OP

Responding *to the* Word

Paul offers ways that we can improve our relationships with others. *Which of his suggestions might I do today?*

Final Thoughts...

FEASTS THIS WEEK

September 28: **St. Wenceslaus
St. Lawrence Riuz
& Companions**

September 29: **St. Michael, St. Gabriel
& St. Raphael**

September 30: **St. Jerome**

October 1: **St. Thérèse of the Child Jesus**

October 2: **The Holy Guardian Angels**

27TH SUNDAY *in* ORDINARY TIME

Everybody knows someone who thinks the world owes them a living. Psychologists call this having a sense of entitlement. A sense of entitlement dulls, or even kills, a person's ability to feel thankful. If I deserve everything I get (or want), there is no room for gratitude.

The plants in the vineyard, the tenants in Jesus' story, and the authorities in Jerusalem seem to have suffered from a sense of entitlement. The ungrateful vines produced sour grapes. The tenants failed to recognize their interdependent partnership with the landlord. The Jerusalem authorities saw their social status as a sign of God's approval, a sign of their salvation. The problem is not that they failed to "earn their keep," it's that their sense of entitlement hobbled their ability to respond with gratitude to what they had received.

The weekly Sunday Eucharist trains us in this attitude. As the Greek name indicates (*eucharistia* = thanksgiving), thanksgiving is at the heart of our Sunday gathering. At the beginning of every eucharistic prayer at every Mass we declare, "It is right and just" to "give thanks to the Lord our God." This is the Church's great prayer of thanks at the banquet table of the Lord. What prayers of thanksgiving do you bring along to Mass today? What fruits do your gifts call you to bring forth to the world? **MARGARET BICK**

Responding *to the* Word

God tends to us like a vineyard owner working to make sure that he will have a good crop. *How have I experienced God's workings in me recently?*

Final Thoughts...

FEASTS THIS WEEK

October 5: **St. Faustina Kowalska**
        Bl. Francis Xavier Seelos

October 6: **Bl. Marie-Rose Durocher**
        St. Bruno

October 7: **Our Lady of the Rosary**

October 9: **St. Denis & Companions**
        St. John Leonardi

28TH SUNDAY *in* ORDINARY TIME

"Go therefore into the main streets, and invite everyone you find to the wedding banquet." These words of Jesus express our prime vocation and our greatest challenge as Christians. We may lament the decrease in number in church attendance and the scarce exposure given by the media to religious issues. But it still remains our responsibility to "go out into the main streets," to reach out to people whoever and wherever they are. Why? To let them know that our God has no other plan for humankind than gathering all peoples together for a banquet, a wedding feast of unmatched magnitude and duration.

"The main streets" of today's world swarm with people hustling and bustling for work, business, shopping, and entertainment. They also abound in people who are jobless, homeless, feeling helpless. The former might have no time even to consider God's invitation to his banquet, and the latter may feel that God ignores their needs and aspirations. Rich or poor, good or bad, they are all in dire need of hearing and experiencing some good news.

In today's Eucharist, may we realize the richness of God's banquet and his deepest desire to see the banquet hall "filled with guests." May we also, in the coming days and weeks, "go into the streets" and share the good news of a munificent God inviting everyone to join the banquet he has prepared for all people.

JEAN-PIERRE PRÉVOST

Responding *to the* Word

Isaiah encourages us to rejoice and be glad for God has saved us. ***How can I thank God today for all God has done for me?***

Final Thoughts...

FEASTS THIS WEEK

October 14: **St. Callistus I**

October 15: **St. Teresa of Jesus**

October 16: **St. Hedwig**
St. Margaret Mary Alacoque

October 17: **St. Ignatius of Antioch**

29TH SUNDAY *in* ORDINARY TIME
World Mission Sunday

In today's first reading, God tells Cyrus, "I call you by your name." I once walked into a church just after Easter and saw a huge banner bearing the words, "Barbara, I have called you by name." My heart skipped a beat! I later learned that "Barbara" was that year's sole RCIA candidate, but for a brief moment the message was mine. God had singled me out! What would he ask of me?

In today's gospel, Matthew tells a story which had political implications in Jesus' time. In an attempt to trap Jesus, the Pharisees questioned whether or not the Jews should be paying taxes to their Roman conquerors. Surely whatever he replied would offend someone. However, Jesus calmly told them: Give God what is God's due and give Caesar what is his due. Jesus' message could be similarly interpreted for our time. We are called to love, honor, and obey God, our Creator. We are also meant to have our feet firmly planted in the world we live in, gifting others with our love, care, and compassion.

God does not call to us with messages splashed across banners. God speaks to us in the silence of our hearts, inviting us to be God's presence in our families, parishes, and communities. If we listen, we will often hear God call us by our name. **BARBARA D'ARTOIS**

Responding *to the* Word

Jesus tells us to give back to God what belongs to God. ***What will I offer back to God today?***

READINGS
OF THE DAY

Isaiah 45.1, 4-6

Psalm 96

1 Thessalonians 1.1-5ab

Matthew 22.15-21

Final Thoughts...

FEASTS THIS WEEK

October 19: **St. John de Brébeuf
St. Isaac Jogues & Companions**

October 20: **St. Paul of the Cross**

October 22: **St. John Paul II**

October 23: **St. John of Capistrano**

October 24: **St. Anthony Mary Claret**

173

30TH SUNDAY *in* ORDINARY TIME

As we approach the end of the Church year, we see Jesus teaching us how to live. The message is simple: love. Love of God, neighbor, and self go hand in hand; one doesn't exist without the other.

Jesus understood how difficult this way of living could be, but he did not compromise. Those who want to follow him must make love their whole life—not just a part, but to love with one's whole heart (compassion), soul (desire), and mind (decision). Love is a decision to give of ourselves and our resources—personal and material—and Jesus expects that our love of God and neighbor will be the center and sum of our lives.

Recently I witnessed a person who was begging on the street receive a coin from a passerby. As they exchanged a greeting, he seemed to pray and give thanks for this gift. Was this a small gift given and received in love? It made me pause and reflect. We all want to be loved and loving.

The daily news shows us how challenging this singular message is. In a world where the word "love" is used to impress, to sell, and even to exert power, Jesus challenges us to see a different way—God's way of love. "I will listen, for I am compassionate" is a great way to sum it all up. **SR. CARMEN DISTON, IBVM**

Responding *to the* Word

God's special compassion is for those most vulnerable who are liable to be victimized by others. ***What can I do to help someone who is vulnerable?***

Final Thoughts...

FEASTS THIS WEEK

October 28: **St. Simon & St. Jude**

ALL SAINTS

Today we celebrate and give thanks for the witness and companionship of those we call the saints. The communion of saints includes, in its broadest sense, not only those formally recognized by the Church but also the exemplary people of faith whom we encounter in our communities and our families. The saints—both those who have gone before us and those who walk among us still—are icons of holiness, windows through which we glimpse the face of God.

All of us are called to holiness, to a life shaped by gospel values. Today's reading of the Beatitudes offers us some guidelines. Bombarded by the lures of consumerism, we are called to be poor in spirit. In a world beset by war and violence, we are called to be peacemakers. In a society that prioritizes competitiveness and ruthless individuality, we are called to be humble. Where grief and discouragement prevail, we are called to be merciful. In the face of injustice, we are invited to "hunger and thirst for righteousness."

Today we pray for the grace to recognize that we are all called to be saints. In the words of the psalm, may we live with "clean hands and pure hearts," as we look forward in hope to sharing in the light of eternal life. **KRYSTYNA HIGGINS**

Responding *to the* Word

The Beatitudes refer to qualities that make for a happier life and that are part of everyone's experience. ***What is one beatitude I need to practice in my life at this time?***

Final Thoughts...

FEASTS THIS WEEK

November 2: **All Souls' Day**
November 3: **St. Martin de Porres**
November 4: **St. Charles Borromeo**

32ND SUNDAY *in* ORDINARY TIME

Most people have had the experience at one time or another of preparing for a journey. It might have been preparing for a vacation; it might have been to visit relatives in other parts of the world. Whatever the reason, generally speaking it was interesting. Every human being is on a journey. For some the journey is short and perhaps colored with tragedy; for others it is a long life filled with periods of good times and bad times, but for all, it is a walk through life toward eternity.

In today's gospel, Matthew uses the example of two young ladies who acted differently in their preparation for meeting the bridegroom. One was completely ready, while the second one had yet to make a needed purchase and as a result she lost the opportunity to accompany the bridegroom when he arrived.

In this example we see the importance of not leaving details to the last minute. No doubt the lesson to be learned from this story of two young ladies is summed up in the words "Be prepared." The whole gospel is directed to the need to be ready to meet the Lord when he calls us to leave this world and enter eternity. Since we have no way of knowing when we will be called to return to the Lord, Jesus warns us to be prepared at all times. **IRIS L. KENDALL**

Responding *to the* Word

Wisdom is found by those who seek her. *Where have I found wisdom in my life? Where do I look for wisdom?*

Final Thoughts...

FEASTS THIS WEEK

November 9: **The Dedication of the Lateran Basilica**

November 10: **St. Leo the Great**

November 11: **St. Martin of Tours**

November 12: **St. Josaphat**

November 13: **St. Frances Xavier Cabrini**

33RD SUNDAY *in* ORDINARY TIME
World Day of the Poor

My balcony overlooks the backyard of a family—three children, two dogs, and a mom and dad. They seem to me an ideal family—the children play together for hours without arguing and help with chores, and the parents appear to have a loving relationship. I often see the husband, and he impresses me. He is a dump-truck driver. Each day, when he returns home, he brushes or hoses off his truck. He is always busy working in the yard, playing with his children, helping his wife hang the laundry, fixing the swing or the basketball hoop, or driving one of his children somewhere. He seems to be a kind of male equivalent of the good wife, described in this Sunday's reading from Proverbs.

In our modern world, marriage partners usually share the work, responsibilities, and privileges of family life, and we know that one need not conform to the images in Proverbs to be a valued marriage partner or to be living a very worthwhile life. What is important is the spirit and dedication with which we employ our gifts for the good of others as we have opportunity.

The readings today celebrate living life fully, using well whatever talents God has entrusted to us. At this point in the Church year, as our attention is drawn to the uncertainty of the end times, it is helpful to hold onto this vision for our lives. And there is a promise: if we do the best we can with what we have, we will find that—as is the case with the faithful servant in the gospel parable—we actually have more to work with. **BETH PORTER**

Responding *to the* **Word**

Paul warns that Jesus' coming will always be a surprise. ***When has Jesus surprised me with an unexpected coming?***

Final Thoughts...

FEASTS THIS WEEK

November 16: **St. Margaret of Scotland**
St. Gertrude

November 17: **St. Elizabeth of Hungary**

November 18: **Dedication of the Basilicas**
of St. Peter & St. Paul
St. Rose Philippine Duchesne

November 21: **The Presentation of**
the Blessed Virgin Mary

185

OUR LORD JESUS CHRIST, KING
of the **UNIVERSE (CHRIST THE KING)**
World Day of Youth

Shepherd? Or king? Which is the model Jesus demonstrates?

A shepherd is one who cares for the sheep, at times even offering even his own life for them. A king, on the other hand, can be remote from most people, unapproachable—and someone whom we may even fear.

But perhaps the two images of shepherd and king are not diametrically opposed. Surely the reason the Church presents them in this same liturgy is to show us new opportunities for understanding Jesus' mission.

When we read about the life of Jesus, we see that his kingdom was not to be understood as one of power, but rather of service. Indeed, Matthew has just reminded us a few verses earlier that "the Son of Man came not to be served, but to serve." This is precisely why, as disciples who seek to imitate Jesus, we embark on the path to eternal life when we give food, clothing, compassion—indeed any assistance—to others. In serving the poor, the sick, and those in prison, we are serving Jesus, for it is in serving "the least of these who are members of my family" that we come to recognize our Lord.

To enter into eternal life, we must follow the example of the shepherd king who did not hesitate to serve, heal, and liberate the poorest of the poor.   **JOSEPH GUNN**

Responding *to the* Word

Our hope for new life means belonging fully to Christ now. ***What can I do to offer myself completely to Christ and his people?***

Final Thoughts...

FEASTS THIS WEEK

November 23: **St. Clement I**
St. Columban
Bl. Miguel Agustín Pro

November 24: **St. Andrew Dũng-Lạc**
& Companions

November 25: **St. Catherine of Alexandria**

November 26: **Thanksgiving Day**

My Spiritual Journey

Know Someone Who Needs a Spiritual Boost?
FREE GIFT SUBSCRIPTION OFFER

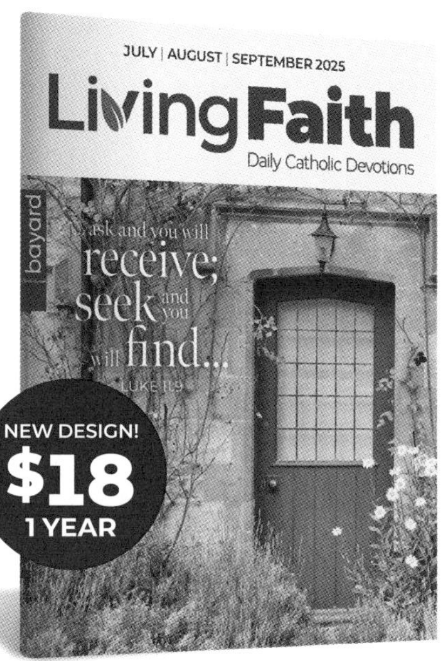

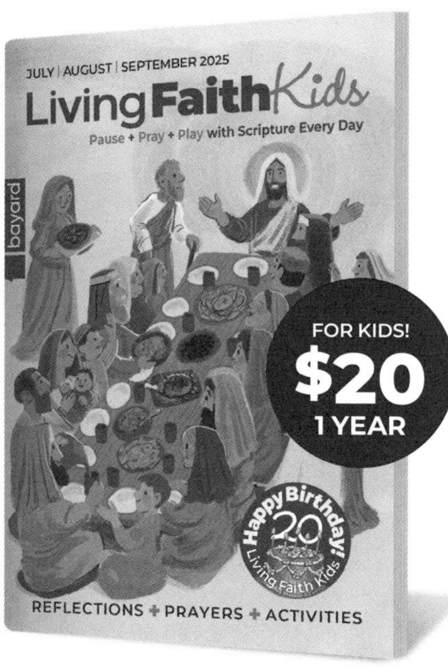

iving Faith encourages daily prayer through imple, faith-filled devotions drawn from the ay's Mass readings.
lso available in large-print – $20/year.

Living Faith Kids nurtures faith in young hearts with daily devotions based on daily Scripture readings, vibrant full-color illustrations and fun activities.

bayard *Living with Christ* is published by Bayard

Code S2510PJG

Call 1-800-246-7390

(Outside U.S. call 937-293-1293) Please refer to promotion code **S2510PJG**
Offer valid for one new gift subscription, must have an active subscription. Expires 11/30/2026

www.livingfaith.com

Your Daily Companion to Prepare and Celebrate the Liturgy
SUBSCRIBE TODAY

$29.95 PER YEAR

For over 85 years, _Living with Christ_ has been a trusted resource for Catholics seeking to deepen their faith and stay connected to the liturgy. This inspiring monthly publication provides everything you need for daily prayer and reflection including daily Mass readings, liturgical insights, monthly calendar and saints feast days and much more!

Whether you're attending Mass in person or praying at home, _Living with Christ_ is your perfect companion for living the Eucharist every day.

Living with Christ is published by Bayard

Code P2510PJ

Call 1-800-214-3386 or visit bayardfaithresources.com